MAR 2 7 2018

THE AMAZING HUMAN BODY

Taste and Digestion

Edited by
Joanne Randolph

Enslow Publishing
101 W. 23rd Street
Suite 240
New York, NY 10011
USA

enslow.com

This edition published ian 2018 by:
Enslow Publishing, LLC.
101 W. 23rd Street, Suite 240
New York, NY 10011

Library of Congress Cataloging-in-Publication Date

Names: Randolph, Joanne, editor.

Title: Taste and digestion / edited by Joanne Randolph.

Description: New York, NY : Enslow Publishing, 2018. | Series: The amazing human body | Audience: Grades 5-8. | Includes bibliographical references and index.

Identifiers: LCCN 2017001986| ISBN 9780766089914 (library-bound) | ISBN 9780766089891 (pbk.) | ISBN 9780766089907 (6-pack)

Subjects: LCSH: Taste—Juvenile literature. | Digestion—Juvenile literature. | Senses and sensation—Juvenile literature.

Classification: LCC QP456 .T36 2018 | DDC 612.8/7—dc23

LC record available at https://lccn.loc.gov/2017001986

Printed in China

CONTENTS

CHAPTER 1

HOW DO WE TASTE?

No, do not bite your little sister to find out. Instead, think about sweet hot fudge . . . salty, crunchy, munchy chips . . . sour, puckery lemons . . . a juicy, meaty hamburger . . . and bitter brewed tea. From these five basic tastes—sweet, salty, sour, savory, bitter—come all the flavors that we humans know and love (or hate). But how do we taste them?

It all starts with your tongue. Check out your tongue in a mirror and notice its soft, velvety texture. Look more closely and you may see that it is actually covered with tiny points of flesh, called papillae, that give it a kind of shag-carpet look. Scattered around, mostly at the front, along the edges, and toward the back, you may see little

All the little bumps on your tongue hold your taste buds. Your teeth and tongue work together to break down the food so it can be swallowed and carried deeper into the digestive system.

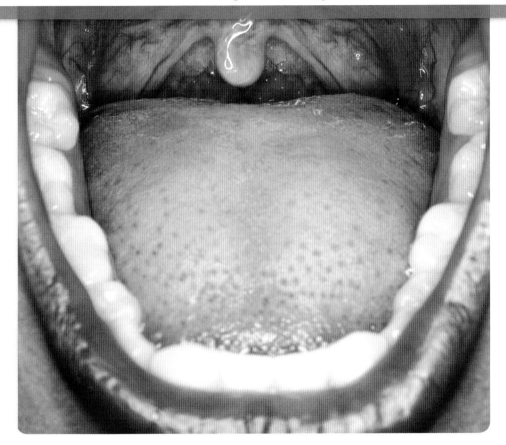

bumps in various shapes. Inside these bumps are your taste buds, each one a collection of cells that are specially equipped to pick up the sweet, sour, bitter, savory, or salty flavors of the food you are chewing. (You also have taste buds on the roof of your mouth and inside your cheeks.) Humans are born with about ten thousand of these tiny taste-bud sense organs, and they work so hard that your body replaces them about every two weeks.

OTHER TASTE BUDDIES

But taste buds don't do all the work. Suppose you are enjoying a spoonful of peanut butter. Remember that shag carpet on your tongue? Each of those tiny tabs of skin is actually designed to help your tongue feel the food in your mouth. They signal wildly to your brain about the thick, smooth, sticky substance that covers them. As

This diagram shows how odors from the air and odors from food are processed. Some odors from food travel to the olfactory bulb from inside the mouth.

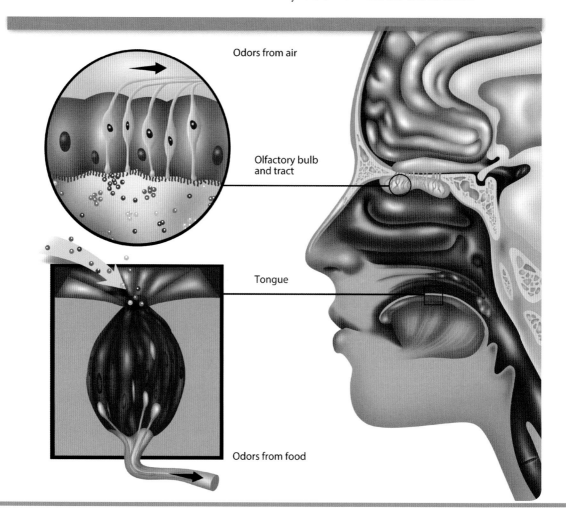

Odors from air

Olfactory bulb and tract

Tongue

Odors from food

you chew, the saliva in your mouth begins to digest the peanut butter with a special chemical. Soon, nothing remains but microscopic particles of peanut butter. These come into contact with your taste buds, where special cells identify the taste of salt and the sweet taste of sugar (which are usually added to peanut butter). Nerves send this information on to your brain. At the same time, molecules carrying the fragrance of the peanut butter waft up through your nose, and scent detectors report the smell to your brain. Almost instantly, your brain gets all these messages and interprets them to recognize the flavor. WOW, it says, PEANUT BUTTER!

The combination of these characteristics—a food's basic tastes, the way it smells, and the feel of it in your mouth, along with its temperature and appearance—gives the food you eat its flavor. Believe it or not, smell accounts for about 85 percent of how something tastes. If you try to eat your peanut butter sandwich while you are holding your nose (which isn't easy), you won't taste much.

WHY TASTE AT ALL?

Why is the tasting process so complicated? Just so we can enjoy our food? There's more to it than that. In all animals, including humans, tasting does two important jobs: it warns us about bad foods and it attracts us to good ones. When our ancient ancestors roamed the forests and fields, hunting and gathering their dinner, they needed a way to tell poisonous plants from healthy ones, or whether a piece of meat was spoiled. In general, toxic plants have a strong bitter flavor that both animals and people know to avoid. Because the taste buds on the back of the tongue are most sensitive to bitterness, even if you start to eat something bad, you have one last chance to gag and spit it out before you swallow. Similarly, spoiled food often

Lemons are a sour food. Typically, lemon is used as a flavoring or is added to other foods rather than being eaten on its own.

tastes sour, warning us not to eat it. Sourness can also mean a food is not ripe and therefore not good to eat.

On the other hand, foods that contain certain amino acids, which are the building blocks of the proteins that our bodies require, have a savory, sort of meaty taste that humans like. Likewise, a pleasant, sweet taste is common in foods that are high in calories, which we need for energy. Early humans learned that sweet and savory tastes meant healthy foods. As a result, we still favor these tastes today. Indeed, human babies are born with a taste for sweetness to make sure that they will eat their first food, milk, which contains natural sugars.

GOOD TASTE—BAD TASTE

The world is full of wonderful things to eat. You probably have favorite foods and others you aren't so fond of. You and your best friend may disagree about what's better: chocolate mint ice cream or caramel vanilla. Why do our tastes differ so much? Tongues and taste buds are all the same, right? And the real stumper: who does like the taste of broccoli anyway?

As scientists try to figure out how our sense of taste works, they are discovering that different people probably taste things differently because they have more or fewer taste buds. Most people, with an average number of buds, are medium tasters and enjoy a range of flavors and foods. (They, most likely, enjoy broccoli.) Certain people can't taste at all, which means that they probably don't enjoy eating anything and so may not be getting enough nutrition through their food. Their tongues have as few as eleven taste buds per square inch.

A third group of people are known as supertasters. These individuals can have one hundred times more taste buds per square inch than nontasters do. This makes them extremely sensitive to certain tastes, and even temperatures, of food. Supertasters don't usually like spicy foods, and bitter or sour foods can have a very strong or unpleasant taste to them. Sweets may be just too rich tasting. Supertasters may not enjoy healthy foods such as grapefruit, broccoli, or celery because the taste is too strong.

FLAVOR WIZARDS

Who puts that cherry flavor in a lollipop or the cheddar-cheese tang in a potato chip? Rest assured, teams of highly trained food chemists known as flavorists toil night and day to bring you all the flavors you crave.

In the lab, flavorists work with hundreds of extracts, powders, and chemicals, some so strong that one drop could flavor an entire swimming pool. Like wizards concocting magic potions, they carefully mix thirty or forty ingredients together, sniffing along the way, until they smell the perfect blend. (Since a flavor is determined mostly by its smell, the flavorists start with the aroma and then tweak the taste.) The flavor can then be applied to chips or ice cream or frozen dinners. After years of such work, flavorists develop finely tuned senses of smell and taste, and like artists, they take pride in their creations. To keep the competition away from their latest banana-barbeque-butterscotch brew, each flavor formula remains top secret.

CHAPTER 2

SENSE OF SWEET

Who doesn't love sweets? From a creamy ice cream cone to a healthy ripe banana, we all love that indescribable yummy sweet taste. But how do we sense sweetness?

As we talked about in the last chapter, a lot happens on your tongue when you take that first bite of sweet, ripe banana. As you chew, your saliva breaks the fruit down into separate molecules. They float into your taste buds, which sit on the little bumps you can see on your tongue. Under a microscope, a taste bud looks like an onion with a small opening at the top. The bud has taste cells in it that contain different kinds of receptors, structures that receive and attach to specific substances. When a food molecule from the banana drops into the taste bud, it fits into its matching receptor, like a key into a lock. This starts a process that sends a signal to the brain, which then tells you there is something sweet on your tongue.

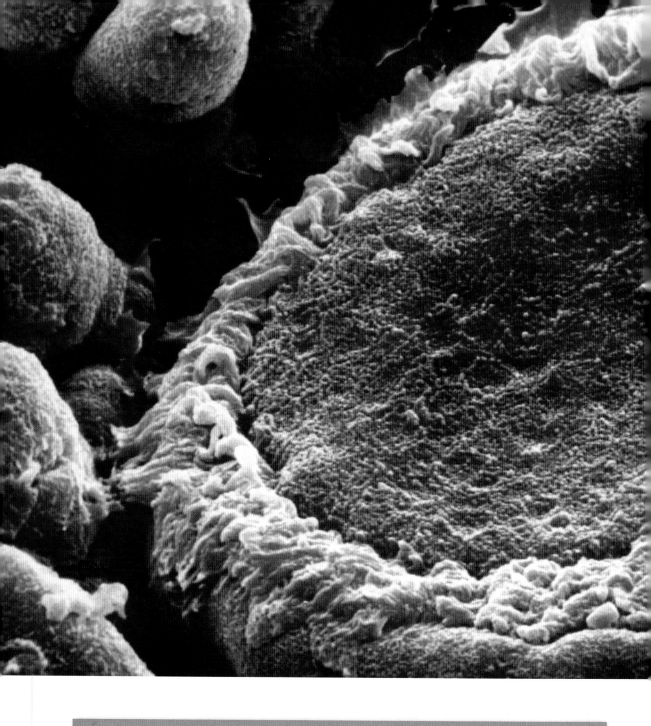

This is a close-up view of a taste bud.

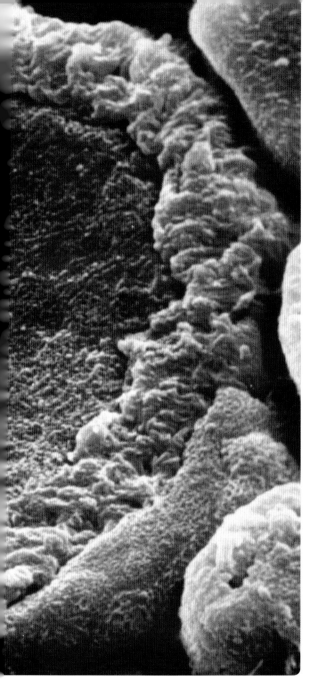

Your mouth contains about ten thousand taste buds. Each has receptors for all five tastes: sweet, sour, bitter, salty, and savory, also called umami (pronounced oo-MOM-ee). A Japanese scientist identified the taste of umami, which we find in meat broth, aged cheese, and many other savory foods. Most foods spark reactions in more than one kind of receptor. For example, a tomato has molecules of sweetness, sourness, saltiness, and umami. As the tomato ripens, the balance changes. There's less sour, more sweet, and more umami.

You might not think a banana is so sweet, but it has more than one kind of natural sugar, and all these sugars fit neatly into the sweet receptors on your tongue. Dr. Karen Yee, a molecular physiologist at the Monell Chemical Senses Center in Philadelphia, explains, "Receptors have their own shape. For the molecule to fit into it, it has to conform to that shape. So a sugar molecule fits into a sweet receptor, whereas a bitter type of molecule has a different shape and doesn't quite fit into that receptor."

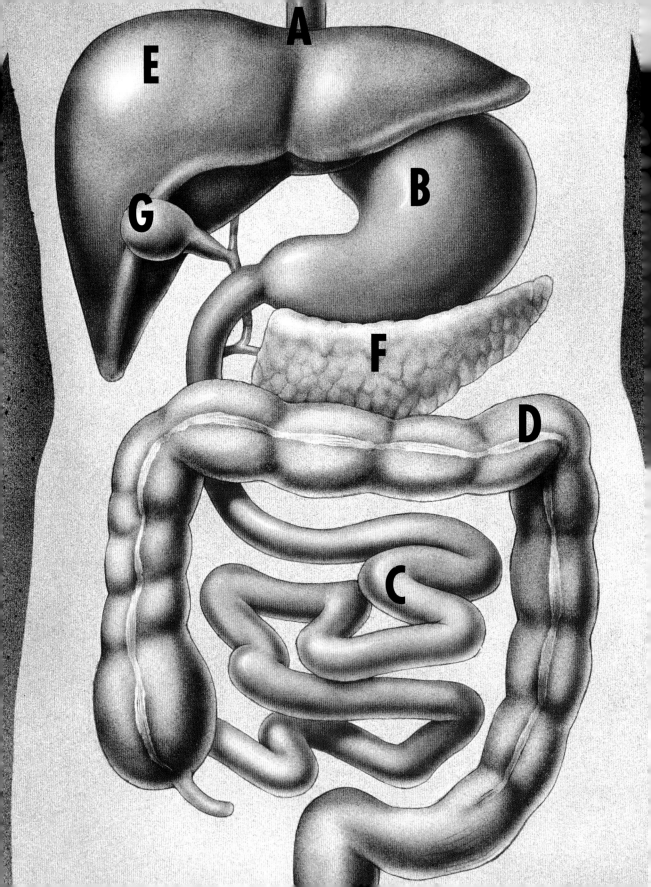

SENSING SWEETNESS

Our understanding of taste has advanced rapidly in recent years. One breakthrough was the discovery that sweet receptors in mammals combine two proteins, labeled T1R2 and T1R3. If either part is missing, the receptor won't respond to sweet molecules. Cats don't have the T1R2 protein and so they have no interest in sweet foods.

The mouth is not the only place where we have mechanisms to detect sweet molecules. Other parts of our digestive system recognize sugars using sensors unlike the receptors in the mouth. Our body turns food we eat into a simple sugar called glucose. "Glucose is really the energy source for our body," says Yee. In our intestines are sensors called glucose transporters that make it possible for glucose to travel into our bloodstream from the digestive organs and from the bloodstream into our cells for use as fuel. Another type of sweet sensor, called a potassium ion channel, allows the pancreas, a gland behind the stomach, to control the level of glucose in the blood.

A TASTE PUZZLE

Yee's colleagues at Monell bred a set of mice that had no T1R3 receptor and then tested their ability to taste sweetness. Yee says, "What they found was that it didn't totally eliminate sweet sensing. The sensation was depressed but, with higher concentrations of sweetness, the mice were able to taste it." This result contradicted what the researchers thought they knew. With just half a T1 receptor,

This diagram shows the digestive system, which includes the mouth (not shown), the esophagus (A), the stomach (B), the small intestine (C), the large intestine (D), as well as the liver (E), pancreas (F), and gall bladder (G).

the mice should not have been sensitive to sweet tastes. The Monell team devised another experiment to explore the mystery.

Their new study found that sweet-sensing taste cells in the mouth contain more than just the T1 receptors. The researchers found that these taste cells also had glucose transporters and potassium ion channels like those in other parts of the body. This explained why the mice without functioning T1 receptors could still taste sweetness, though at a much reduced level.

Have you ever eaten something very sugary, such as a piece of pecan pie, and felt as though you couldn't look at another sweet dessert? The Monell scientists suggest that perhaps the potassium ion channel in your tongue's sweet taste cells are acting the way they would in the pancreas. Sensing the overload of calories, they signal that no more are needed.

WHY ARE SWEET FOODS SO APPEALING?

Our earliest ancestors could not be sure of their food supply. Hunting and gathering took energy, and finding calorie-rich foods helped them survive. So they developed a preference for sweet and fatty foods. We've inherited that trait, whether it's useful for us or not.

It can be useful during times of rapid growth. Compared to adults, children like sweeter foods. Monell scientist Dr. Danielle Reed found a connection between periods of bone growth in young people and their desire for very sweet foods. As bone growth slows and the need for extra calories declines, so does fondness for highly sweet foods. Teens eventually come to prefer lower levels of sweetness in what they eat.

There were no grocery stores where prehistoric people could pop in and buy dinner. They had to hunt and gather all their food.

Our hunting-and-gathering ancestors didn't always have sweet fruits at their disposal. In their quest for calories, it would have been useful for them to be able to detect sweetness at low levels in starchy plants. A recent study suggests that sensitivity to sweetness varies with a population's location. It appears that people living in the tropics tend to be less able to taste sweetness at low concentrations compared to people in higher latitudes. A possible explanation is that most plants with really high levels of sugar come from the tropics and even people with low sensitivity to sweet tastes would be attracted to them. Outside the tropics, people might need a greater sensitivity to sugars to find energy-rich food plants appetizing.

TRICKING THE TASTE BUDS

Imagine squeezing a lemon into your mouth and thinking it's lemonade. That's what happens if you chew a "miracle berry" before squeezing the lemon. The fruit of a shrub that grows in West Africa, the berry contains a protein that affects the taste buds. In

The miracle berry may not look like much, but it could have a big impact on the food industry and the kinds of food we eat.

the presence of acid, this protein, miraculin, binds to the sweet receptors on your tongue. It causes any sour thing you eat or drink to taste miraculously sweet. A tomato turns into tomato candy and unsweetened cranberry juice becomes cranberry punch. The effect lasts for about an hour.

In Africa, people have used it for centuries to sweeten palm wine and other sour food and drinks. In Japan, it's popular among people with diabetes because it allows them to have sweets without the damage sugar would cause. There are cafés in Japan that serve a miracle berry followed by low-calorie, sour desserts that, under the influence of miraculin, taste like any sugar-laden treat.

A team of chefs in Chicago is experimenting with the berries. One of them uses the berry to make his homemade sugar-free pancake syrup seem like maple syrup. They see miraculin as a tool for reducing world hunger. If it were available in large enough quantities, it could make plants that are unpleasantly sour seem tasty to people who need the calories.

Japanese scientists are working on creating lettuce and tomatoes that produce the miraculin protein. If they're successful, it could be the route to a cheap worldwide supply.

THERE'S MORE TO THE TONGUE THAN MEETS THE EYE

Our tongues play a key role in our survival. First they make eating pleasurable by recognizing good tastes. They also guard us against eating unsafe food by recognizing bad tastes. They move our food around our mouth and push it into a place for swallowing. But they

This diagram shows the structural details of a papilla and taste bud. Although one of the tongue's main functions is tasting, scientists believe the tongue may perform more complicated tasks they have yet to uncover.

TASTE BUD

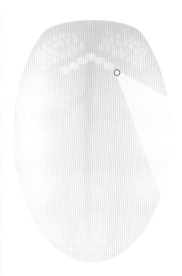

Tongue

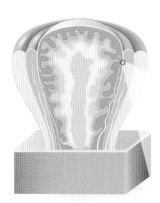

Papilla

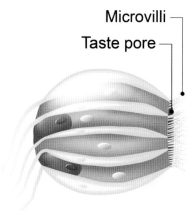

Microvilli
Taste pore

Taste bud

might have greater responsibilities that we're not aware of. Perhaps some of the sweet-sensors found in the taste cells aid in moving glucose into the bloodstream. Perhaps other sensors make eating a sugary food less pleasurable once our glucose levels are high enough.

Yee says, "We think of the tongue as a tasting thing, but it might play a more complex role. It's much more complicated than just sensing sweet or salty or bitter or sour. We're hoping that what we learn might help in controlling obesity and diabetes. But much still needs to be discovered."

Artichokes change the chemistry in the mouth for a little while, making things that are not sweet taste like they are.

TASTE-CHANGING CHEMICALS

So miraculin makes sour and bitter things taste sweet. Are there other taste-changing chemicals out there? There are! Have you ever tried to drink a glass of orange juice right after brushing your teeth? If your toothpaste contains sodium lauryl sulfate, the juice can taste terrible. That's because sodium lauryl sulfate, which is widely used in toothpaste to make it foam, temporarily disables the sweet receptors on your tongue. With the orange juice's sweetness blocked, the natural sourness and bitterness of the juice are exaggerated.

Other taste modifiers are found in artichokes. Just after eating fresh artichokes a majority of people find that water tastes sweet. Artichokes contain two chemicals that temporarily alter the tongue, making nonsweet substances seem sweet.

CHAPTER 3

GRIND, GULP, AND GURGLE!

So now we understand a bit more about how we taste and why some things taste better to us than others. But what happens to our food after we put it in our mouths. Let's follow the food as it journeys through the human digestive system!

So, here we go. Let's say it's seven o'clock on Monday morning. You're probably looking forward to a day of math and social studies, maybe a spelling test, some laughs with friends, books to read, and people to see. Perhaps you have a soccer game later. Whew. You'll need lots of energy to get through the day, so your body stays busy too, making fuel to keep you going. It all starts at breakfast.

GRIND

Those Fiber-Crunch-Os you eat every day have a long way to go—approximately 30 feet (9 meters)—through the twists and turns of your digestive system. On the way, your body removes all the nutrients it needs to survive. The whole process can take around twenty-four hours.

Digestion starts the minute you take a bite. Your teeth grind up the food, and saliva (which contains enzymes to help soften and

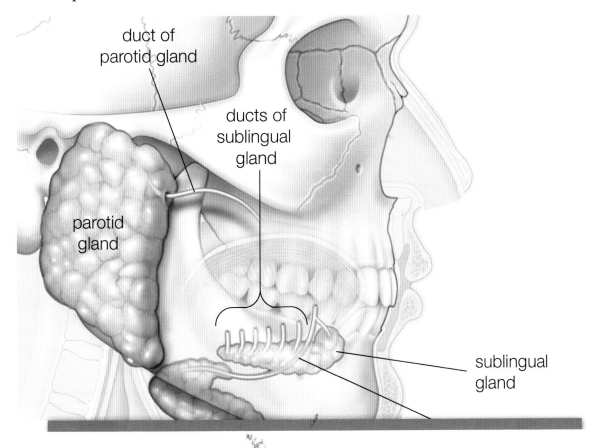

duct of
parotid gland

ducts of
sublingual
gland

parotid
gland

sublingual
gland

This diagram shows the salivary glands, which produce the saliva your mouth needs to help break down foods.

break down your crunchy cereal) mixes in to create a mouthful of mush. This mush is called a bolus, and after plenty of chewing (don't skimp on this step), it is ready to leave your mouth and begin its journey into your stomach.

GULP

Now your tongue pushes the bolus around to the back of your mouth, where muscles in your throat take over. The throat is a busy place. Down the front is the passageway to your lungs (sometimes called the windpipe) through which you breathe. And at the very back of the throat is an opening into your nose to let the air in and out. As you swallow, this entryway closes up. At the same time, a

The esophagus is a long tube made out of muscle that expands and contracts to move the food you swallow toward your stomach.

flap of skin falls over the windpipe to prevent food from "going down the wrong way" and into your lungs.

Let's say that bite made it safely past the booby traps in your throat. Powerful muscles in your esophagus, a stretchy 10-inch (25.4-centimeter) tube, push the bolus past the lungs and rib cage and on into your stomach, where the real work begins.

GURGLE

The stomach is a dark and dangerous place, if you are a mouthful of mushed-up food. At rest, it is just an empty sack; its muscular lining, or stomach wall, is covered with rolls, folds, and wrinkles.

The stomach has thick layers of muscle. If it didn't make a slippery slime called mucus, the stomach would digest itself.

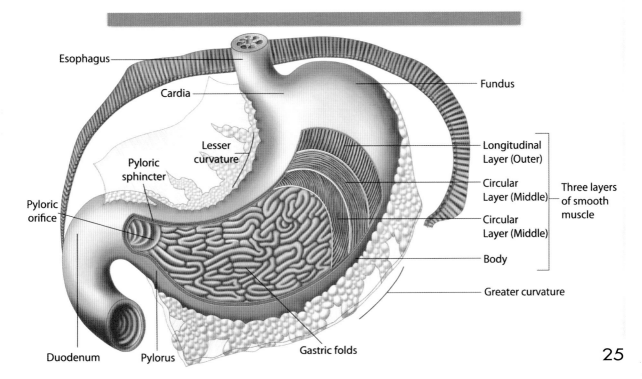

Esophagus

Cardia

Lesser curvature

Pyloric sphincter

Pyloric orifice

Fundus

Longitudinal Layer (Outer)

Circular Layer (Middle)

Circular Layer (Middle)

Body

Three layers of smooth muscle

Greater curvature

Duodenum   Pylorus

Gastric folds

Once it contains food—and it can hold than a gallon (about four liters)—it stretches out and becomes a gurgling, churning, sloshing, digesting machine. Stomach muscles squash and squeeze food into smaller pieces. Special cells in the stomach lining release stomach juices, including strong acid, to continue breaking down the food into a thick, soupy liquid.

It can take the stomach up to four hours to break down greasy foods. Your breakfast cereal probably takes an hour or so.

GUTS

Now things get twisted. Really. The stomach slowly releases the soupy mixture, called chyme, into the twisty, turny tube called the small intestine. At about 22 feet (6.7 m) long, the only way it can fit inside you is to wind tightly back and forth. Why so long? The small intestine (or gut, if you prefer) has a lot of work to do, so it needs all that length. Special digestive juices that break down the starches and proteins in your breakfast enter the small intestine as needed from an organ called the pancreas. The liver provides bile to help dissolve fats. When their work is through, your breakfast is nothing but a clear liquid.

Okay, so how does the food we eat fuel our bodies? That comes next. Like the stomach, most of the small intestine is all wrinkly inside, and the wrinkles are covered with teeny-weeny, wiggly, fingerlike villi. Cells on the villi gobble up the nutrients in your now-liquid breakfast and pass them into tiny blood vessels in the walls of the gut. From here, the nutrients travel throughout the body, riding along in your bloodstream and delivering meals to all your parts: organs, bones, nerves, muscles, and brain.

The large intestine is on the outside of the diagram. The small intestine winds its way around in the center here.

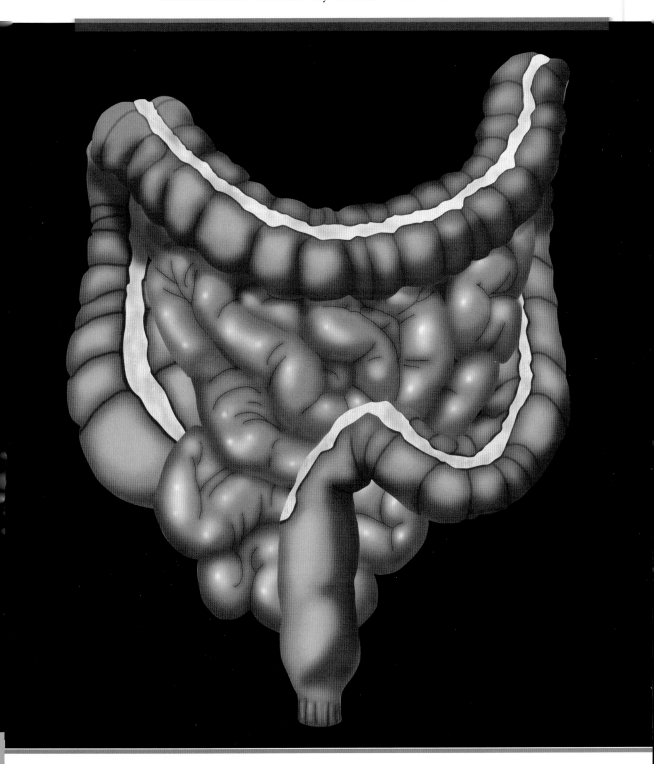

It must be almost lunchtime by now, since food remains in the small intestine about four hours before it passes into the large intestine, which is wider, but shorter (about 5 feet [1.5 m] long). Very little remains of your breakfast; most has been digested and distributed throughout the body. The large intestine, or bowel, absorbs remaining water and vitamins. What's left moves slowly through the bowel and, over five or ten or even eighteen hours, hardens into a mass of small amounts of undigested food, dead cells from the gut, a small bit of water, and bacteria. In fact, your bowel contains about one hundred trillion bacteria, friendly critters that clean your large intestine by eating what cannot be digested. This mass, called feces (you may know it as poop), is now ready to leave your body.

GO!

By now it's probably seven o'clock on Tuesday morning. You are looking forward to another busy day. You'll need another bowl of Fiber-Crunch-Os for breakfast. But first, perhaps a stop in the bathroom. . . .

STOMACH WITH A VIEW

In 1822, fur trapper Alexis St. Martin was seriously wounded by a shotgun and not expected to live. Hoping for the best, Dr. William Beaumont patched him up. Amazingly, St. Martin healed. But there was one problem: a two-inch (five-centimeter) hole into his stomach wouldn't close over. Beaumont was delighted (St. Martin was not)—he could see everything going on inside! At that time, no one understood how digestion worked. Did the stomach cook or grind food? Or did it use chemicals to dissolve food? For twelve years, Beaumont studied the contents of St. Martin's stomach. He tied food to a string and put it in through the stomach hole and pulled it out, and he noted the movements of the stomach walls. He became famous for describing the way stomach acid helps to digest food. As for St. Martin, he eventually married, had children, and lived to the ripe old age of eighty-three. The hole in his stomach never healed.

GETTING THERE IS HALF THE FUN

Muscles around your esophagus tighten and release in a wavelike motion to push each bite of food down into your stomach. This automatic process is called peristalsis. Each bolus takes two or three seconds to make the trip. Your esophageal muscles are so powerful that you can even swallow standing on your head (astronauts do it), although we wouldn't recommend it. What happens when you throw up? Reverse peristalsis, of course, which pushes the food and liquid out of your stomach, back up the esophagus, and out.

What about pee? As your blood delivers nutrients from your digestive system to the rest of your body, it collects wastes in return. Then the blood arrives at your two kidneys, where tiny filters clean it. On it goes, and the waste drips into your bladder as urine, or pee. As your bladder reaches half full, you can begin to plan your next trip to the bathroom.

More than 2 gallons (7.6 L) of liquid rush through your gut each day, some at 500 miles (805 kilometers) per hour.

With all its wrinkles and villi, the surface area of your gut is 2,000 square feet (186 square meters), the size of baseball diamond, more than eighty times the surface of your skin!

CHAPTER 4

WIPEOUT!

Remember those bacteria we talked about that aid in digestion? What if you found out that modern medicine is killing them? Antibiotics have saved countless lives and relieved untold suffering since their first use. But now there's a suspicion they may be behind some of the more troubling health problems in the country. Dr. Martin Blaser, of New York University's Langone Medical Center, is worried that overuse of antibiotics is causing the substantial increase in such conditions as allergies, asthma, diabetes, and obesity.

This image shows a few different kinds of gut bacteria, such as *Staphylococcus,
Enterococcus,* and *Lactobacillus,* that help us break down our food.

KILLING THE GOOD ALONG WITH THE BAD

Blaser notes that the average child in the United States has had ten to twenty courses of antibiotics by the age of eighteen. The problem is that antibiotics wipe out not just bad bacteria but also good bacteria. We have trusted that when we stop taking antibiotics our gut flora go back to their normal state. But Blaser's lab has found that sometimes our helpful flora never really recover from a course of antibiotics. Our gut microbiota become less diverse, and some of the missing microbes may be the ones that offer protection against immune-system disorders.

Farmers have long known that giving their livestock small doses of antibiotics causes them to gain weight. Could this be behind our obesity epidemic? In Blaser's laboratory they've found that treating mice with low-dose antibiotics, similar to what farm animals get, results in significant increases in body fat. The same is true when they give them high doses, similar to what children get for infections.

This is a milking machine. Drinking milk from cows that have been treated with antibiotics may contribute to the obesity epidemic in the United States.

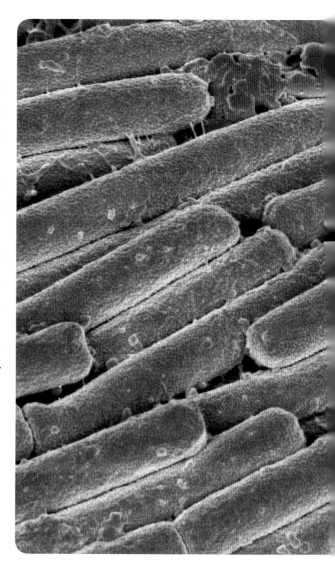

We're subjected to antibiotics not just when our doctors prescribe them. Scientists have also found trace amounts in milk and meat. What might this constant exposure be doing to our microbiota?

Blaser suggests a couple of alternatives to the kind of antibiotic therapy we have now. One would be to develop antibiotics that target a very narrow range of harmful bacteria, leaving intact the beneficial ones. Another approach would be to reinforce the good bacteria so that they could overwhelm the bad bacteria. The ecological balance would be restored.

NOT FOR THE SQUEAMISH

Clostridium difficile (*C. diff*) is a gut microbe to beware of. It's common for people to carry it unknowingly in their intestine without a problem. However, it's a bacterium that will take over if given the chance. And when it does, the infection can be serious, even deadly.

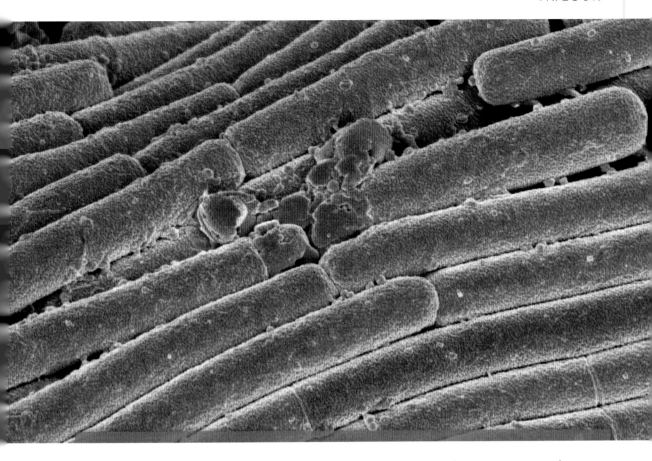

The long, greenish, rod-shaped objects in this scanning electron micrograph (SEM) are the *Clostridium difficile* bacteria, which causes illness.

Most often that happens after a course of antibiotics, which can't tell the good intestinal bugs from the bad bugs. When antibiotics kill off harmless gut bacteria, *C. diff* bacteria multiply. A *C. diff* infection causes diarrhea, vomiting, pain, and fever. Many patients have to be hospitalized. If they're lucky, a course of antibiotics aimed at *C. diff* will cure the infection. But some people never fully recover, suffering from repeated bouts of illness.

For those desperate enough, there's a pretty reliable cure. It involves transplanting poop from a healthy donor into the sick person. Dr. Catherine Lozupone, a microbiologist at the University of Colorado in Denver, says, "It's not the nicest thing to think about but it's extremely effective." In a controlled, randomized study in the Netherlands, fifteen out of sixteen people were cured by this method. By contrast, of the twenty-six patients in the study who were treated with antibiotics instead, only seven were cured.

Lozupone says, "This proves the concept that it's the whole community of healthy bacteria that can fight off the invading bacteria. The ideal situation is that we would know exactly which combination of probiotic bacteria to use, rather than just using this bunch of bacteria together in a fecal sample. . . . The field is moving toward trying to get a better understanding of which are the protective bacteria that help to fight off things like C. diff infections."

A recent study at Canada's University of Calgary tested the effectiveness of pills containing fecal bacteria. For this trial, researchers processed poop from donors—usually family members of patients—until it contained only bacteria. They encased the bacteria in three layers of gelatin capsule to make sure it made it out of the stomach and into the intestine alive. The patients swallowed between twenty-four and thirty-four capsules each. All twenty-seven participants in the study were cured.

CHAPTER 5

FOOD AT WORK

Your body needs food for energy. Your digestive system works to break down those foods so that our bodies can access the vitamins and other nutrients. Vitamins are like tools. They don't work by themselves but with other nutrients. They keep you from getting sick and help turn food into energy. Fruits and vegetables are good sources of vitamins.

Your body factory uses proteins to build and repair itself. Your body can't store extra protein, so you don't need to eat big servings of such foods as meat, eggs, beans, or nuts, but you do need to eat them regularly.

In factories materials like wood, metal, cloth, and plastic are used to make all kinds of things, from cars to toys to sofas. Your body is like a factory, but it uses nutrients in food to make—you!

The most important nutrients in food are carbohydrates, proteins, fats, vitamins, minerals, and water. Factories need power to work. Your body factory gets the energy it needs from carbohydrates found in bread, cereal, pasta, rice, potatoes, and fruit. Fats are also a source of energy and form a protective layer under our skin to keep us warm. Vitamins and minerals help convert food into energy, boost the immune system, and help cells and organs function properly, among many other tasks. Water carries food and other things to every part of your body factory. Every factory has to get rid of trash and waste. Whatever food your body doesn't use or store gets passed out as urine and feces.

BUILDING YOUR PLATE

So how do you know which foods to eat to stay healthy? Remember the Food Pyramid? Maybe not. That visual guide to eating well was replaced by something simpler-looking in 2011, when the US Department of Agriculture (USDA), in collaboration with first lady Michelle Obama, introduced the new MyPlate Program. This collaboration started in response to a 2010 report of the White House Childhood Obesity Task Force. This report challenged the USDA to design a new symbol to inspire Americans to eat healthier.

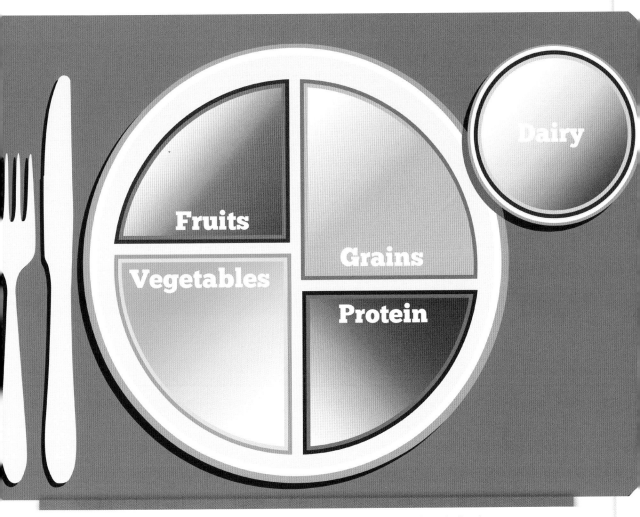

The MyPlate diagram tells us about how much of each food group we need at each meal. We need more vegetables and grains and smaller amounts of protein, fruits, and dairy.

WHAT IS MYPLATE?

The MyPlate icon shows a plate with the five food groups and suggests what the portions should be for each group. This visual aid is meant to make it easier to picture the portions when serving dinner, for example. The USDA stated on the one-year anniversary of MyPlate's release that it was launched "to encourage people to think about their food choices in order to lead healthier lifestyles. . . . Today we celebrate the great strides we are making from our local schools to the dinner table as Americans embrace MyPlate and find practical ways to apply it to their daily lives."

HEALTHY EATING PLATE VS. MYPLATE

In response to MyPlate's launching, the Harvard School of Public Health and Harvard Medical School created the Healthy Eating Plate. The Harvard group suggested that its graphic was preferable because it was based on the best available science and was not subjected to political pressure from food lobbyists. Walter Willet, chair of the department of nutrition at Harvard School of Public Health, said, "Unfortunately, like earlier US Department of Agriculture Pyramids, MyPlate mixes science with the influence of powerful agricultural interests, which is not the recipe for healthy eating."

Harvard's Healthy Eating Plate examines each of the five food groups in depth. It also addresses issues MyPlate doesn't, such as whole grains vs. refined carbohydrates, protein sources, healthy oils, hydration, and exercise.

How Refined Is that Carbohydrate?

Refined grains like white bread and white rice act similar to sugar in the body. Eating too much of these refined carbohydrates may contribute to weight gain and increase the risk of diabetes. The Healthy Eating Plate emphasizes whole grains such as whole wheat bread and brown rice.

HEALTHY PLATE

1/2 VEGETABLES & FRUIT

Choose variety of colors. Green, yellow orange and red are the best choices

1/4 GRAIN FOOD

Try to avoid refined (white) grains and prefer whole (brown) grains

1/4 PROTEIN

Fish, poultry, nuts, dairy are ideal sources of protein

WATER

Avoid sugary drinks

The Healthy Plate guideline is more specific than MyPlate and takes into account the latest findings about nutrition and human health.

PROTEIN DOESN'T JUST MEAN MEAT

The second issue Healthy Eating Plate addresses that MyPlate does not is protein quality. Many foods can supply your body with protein, but how they affect the body differs. The Healthy Eating Plate encourages consumers to choose fish, poultry, beans, or nuts because they contain healthy forms of protein. It also encourages consumers to avoid processed meat, such as hot dogs, and limit the intake of red meat, a source of saturated fat. According to the Centers for Disease Control, "Diets high in saturated fat have been linked to chronic disease, specifically, coronary heart disease. The Dietary Guidelines for Americans 2010 recommend consuming less than 10 percent of daily calories as saturated fat."

HEALTHY OILS

MyPlate does not address fat or oils. The Healthy Eating Plate depicts a bottle of healthy oil. Unsaturated oils—considered fats our bodies need—include olive, canola, and other plant oils and fats found naturally in fish. These healthy oils are good for the heart.

EAT, DRINK, AND BE ACTIVE

A final difference between the Healthy Eating Plate and MyPlate is what each recommends to drink. MyPlate recommends dairy at every meal. However, the developers of the Healthy Eating Plate say that there is no evidence that high dairy intake protects against bone disease and that Americans should drink more water, coffee, or tea, because they are naturally calorie free. The Healthy Eating Plate also reminds its audience that half the secret to weight control is exercise.

People who are active have healthier digestive systems—and healthier bodies in general.

Foods such as yogurt, fruit, and vegetables are what your bacteria like.

WHAT SHOULD YOU EAT?

With all of the conflicting messages, what should you believe? MyPlate and the Healthy Eating Plate share general outlines for healthy eating. The major difference is that the Healthy Eating Plate is more specific about what the evidence says about the effect of dietary choices on your health. In general, try to make healthy choices to keep your digestive system, and the rest of your body, healthy, too!

bolus A ball of chewed up food that travels down your esophagus and into your stomach.

calories The amount of energy needed to raise the temperature of water 1 °C.

chyme Food broken down into a thick, soupy liquid in the stomach.

Clostridium difficile (*C. diff*) A bacterium normally found in gut that, when it overgrows, can cause symptoms such as diarrhea or inflammation of the large intestine.

flavorist A food chemist who creates flavors to add to foods.

liver A large organ in the abdomen that is involved in many metabolic processes.

lobbyist A person who tries to influence laws or lawmakers.

microbiota Microorganisms living in the human body.

microscopic So small it is only visible using a microscope.

molecule The smallest particle that something can be divided into without changing its chemical properties.

nerve A fiber that carries signals throughout the body.

organ A part in an organism that has a specific, important job to do, such as the heart or the liver.

pancreas A gland behind the stomach that aids in digestion and other processes.

peristalsis The automatic wavelike motion of the smooth muscles of the digestive tract that pushes food through.

potassium ion channel A pathway that allows potassium to pass through, but that blocks other ions.

saliva A watery liquid produced in the mouth by glands that aids in chewing, swallowing, and digestion.

toxic Poisonous; deadly; harmful.

villi Fingerlike projections on a surface of the small intestine that absorb nutrients.

BOOKS

Canavan, Thomas. *Fueling the Body: Digestion and Nutrition*. New York, NY: PowerKids Press, 2015.

Conklin, Wendy. *Digestion and Using Food*. Huntington Beach, CA: Teacher Created Materials, 2015.

Gomdori co. *Survive! Inside the Human Body, Vol. 1: The Digestive System*. San Francisco, CA: No Starch Press, 2013.

Mason, Paul. *Your Growling Guts and Dynamic Digestive System*. New York, NY: Crabtree Publishing, 2015.

Towne, Isobel, and Jennifer Viegas. *The Mouth and Nose in 3D*. New York, NY: Rosen Central, 2015.

WEBSITES

KidsHealth, What Are Taste Buds?
kidshealth.org/en/kids/taste-buds.html
Discover more details about taste buds.

National Institute of Diabetes and Digestive and Kidney Diseases
www.niddk.nih.gov/health-information/health-topics/Anatomy/your-digestive-system/Pages/anatomy.aspx
This governmental website provides more information about the digestive system, including what happens to the digested food and how digestion is controlled.

TeensHealth, Digestive System
kidshealth.org/en/teens/digestive-system.html
Learn more about the digestive system and how it works.

INDEX